Affirmations
for
BLACK WOMEN
A JOURNAL

100+ Positive Messages and Prompts
to Affirm Your Self-Worth,
Empower Your Spirit,
& Attract Success

Oludara Adeeyo
Author of *Self-Care for Black Women*

ADAMS MEDIA
New York   London   Toronto   Sydney   New Delhi

Adams Media
An Imprint of Simon & Schuster, Inc.
100 Technology Center Drive
Stoughton, Massachusetts 02072

First Adams Media hardcover edition
December 2022

ADAMS MEDIA and colophon are
trademarks of Simon & Schuster.

For information about special discounts for
bulk purchases, please contact Simon &
Schuster Special Sales at 1-866-506-1949 or
business@simonandschuster.com.

The Simon & Schuster Speakers Bureau can
bring authors to your live event. For more
information or to book an event contact
the Simon & Schuster Speakers Bureau
at 1-866-248-3049 or visit our website at
www.simonspeakers.com.

Interior design by Priscilla Yuen
Illustrations by Tess Armstrong
Interior images © Simon & Schuster, Inc.

Manufactured in the United States of
America

2 2023

ISBN 978-1-5072-2019-1

Dedicated to Black women.
May this journal empower you to continue
your self-care journey.

Acknowledgments

Foremost, thank you to everyone who supported my first book, *Self-Care for Black Women*. It has been amazing to see many Black women begin to embrace self-care as a daily practice. My deepest desire is that you also enjoy *Affirmations for Black Women: A Journal*. Affirmations and journaling have been a pinnacle part of my self-healing journey. The evolvement into my Black womanhood included many days of writing in my journal and using affirmations to rebuild my confidence and self-love. Next, thank you to everyone at Adams Media and Simon & Schuster who worked on this project. Your continued effort to manage this subject matter with extreme care is greatly appreciated. And to my family and friends who continue to be the battery pack in my back that pushes me forward with my writing and other professional endeavors, thank you. I love you all.

Contents

Introduction

Affirmations are powerful positive statements that you use to speak over your life. Not only will they change the way you think but they will also transform your living experience. Using affirmations allows you to shift your mindset from negative to positive thinking. Additionally, affirmations help boost your self-confidence, self-trust, and self-love—elements you need to manifest your desires. As you begin to love and trust yourself more, you will loosen the tight grip on how you think your life should look and lean into the unknowingly good things your God and the universe wants for you.

Practicing affirmations is essential to your radical self-care journey. As Black women, we tend to internalize the racist and sexist ideologies that are spewed about us in society—meaning we take hold of the negative energy from things like microaggressive experiences and let them live in our mind, body, and soul. You begin to believe the derogatory messages about Black women. This then causes you to create false beliefs about yourself, which lead to things like self-doubt, self-sabotage, and low self-worth.

Sis, you are more than enough and deserving of a life filled with love, peace, and joy. Affirmations can get you there. Using positive mantras to reconfigure the way you think about yourself and your life will help you practice manifestation. You will attract the life of your dreams. And while positive thinking is part of manifesting, it's not the only piece. You must be intentional and clear about your desires, unabashedly ask your higher power for them, write them down, take action toward those goals, maintain a spirit of gratitude, and let go of limiting beliefs as to how or when what you're manifesting will arrive. This process can start with using the affirmation prompts in *Affirmations for Black Women: A Journal*. You will declare something positive over your life and then write out your intentions, goals, and thoughts around the affirmation in order to make it happen. It's all about introducing your mind to a higher vibrational level of thinking.

There are many ways to use positive statements to elevate your life. You can start your day by saying affirmations out loud to yourself every morning, such as, *I am going to have a good day*. The affirmations you find in this journal can be said once or as many times as you need throughout the day. The simple act of journaling about your affirmation will help you figure out how the affirmation uniquely applies to you while also cementing its validity in your mind.

In *Affirmations for Black Women: A Journal*, you will find more than one hundred affirmations with journal prompts that focus on every aspect of your life, including your emotional, mental, and physical health, as well as affirmations for your practical, professional, and social life. Use this journal as a way to incorporate affirmations into your daily self-care practice. A life filled with abundance is calling you.

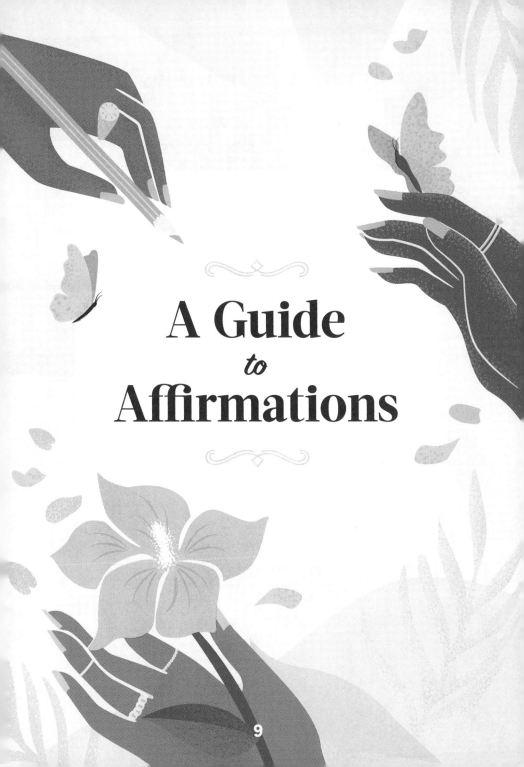

A Guide
to
Affirmations

What Are Affirmations?

Affirmations are simple statements that empower you to change the way you think and feel about yourself. They are one of the most common self-help techniques. While affirmations are phrases that encourage you to think more positively, they are not to be confused with toxic positivity—which means using positive statements to invalidate the reality of a situation. With affirmations, you are acknowledging your present while affirming your future.

Generally, affirmations are written in the present tense, as if you already have these things. For example, if you are in the middle of job searching, you might use the following affirmation: *I am employed.* Or perhaps you are struggling with your self-esteem; you might use this affirmation: *I am confident.* This gets your mind and spirit in the realm of what you are already calling in for the future.

Research has found that affirmations are powerful because they help improve your mental health by altering your response to psychological stress. Most of us have a great view of self, but when we encounter situations that cause us to question our worth and capability, we create defense mechanisms that hinder our personal growth and performance. Affirmations operate as a shield between your inner self and society by combating any negative coping skills or beliefs about self that you've created as a response to trauma. The more you use affirmations, the less vulnerable you are to stress, and the healthier thoughts, feelings, and behaviors you experience.

Why Are Affirmations Important for Black Women?

Affirmations are important for Black women because it is an essential tool that can help you heal from the effects of misogynoir, a.k.a. racism and sexism, that is targeted at Black women. Starting in childhood, Black women experience microaggressions that have a great impact on how we think about ourselves. We are constantly fed messages that tell us we are less than, the way we look is not ideal, the way we talk is wrong, the way our hair comes naturally out of our head is unpleasant, the way our bodies are shaped is unnatural, the color of our skin is not desirable, and the list goes on. We are told that our existence is a problem and, because of this, we internalize a lot of these discriminatory messages.

When you internalize something, this means you have allowed that thing to unconsciously become a part of your identity. And for Black women, so much of our identity is tied to how we are perceived in this world. So, when we are constantly berated with negative notions about our personhood, we begin to believe them—causing race-based traumatic stress. This is a mental injury caused by any negative racial encounter. For example, if you're constantly being told that your hair is ugly or that it is hard to deal with, you will believe this and become self-conscious about your hair—possibly taking drastic measures to alter it or hide it to avoid ridicule.

Additionally, dismantling the chains of internalized racism is an imperative part of a self-care journey for a Black woman. When you use affirmations, this helps you unpack and unlearn every bad thing that you have been made to believe about yourself. Healing starts from within, and your brain has the capacity to reroute its negative thinking. This is called neuroplasticity, which speaks to your brain's ability to reconfigure after obtaining new information—like positive affirmations.

It is mentally exhausting to be a Black woman in society, knowing that a majority of society dislikes your existence. You feel lonely, like no one cares about you—a very isolating emotion. However, you can't sit there. It'll only hold you back from fulfilling your life's calling. Affirmations allow Black women to create a new relationship with the most important person in our lives: ourselves. This new bond will improve self-esteem and motivation.

How to Incorporate Affirmations Into Your Life and Daily Practice

The point of including affirmations as a part of everyday self-care is that it will encourage you to continue shifting your mind to a positive way of thinking while acknowledging the reality of your circumstances. This helps you stay grounded. Additionally, it is important that you continuously meditate on the affirmations that you choose to use. Here, "meditate" simply means to think deeply and focus on whatever that affirmation is trying to help you manifest.

Here are some of the many ways that you can integrate affirmations into your life. Include them in your daily routine:

- Use the affirmations in this book, writing about them in this journal and processing your thoughts around each affirmation. Writing it down is one of the best ways to incorporate affirmations into your everyday life.

- Choose an affirmation that you will focus on and think about in your quiet time. "Quiet time" here is five or more minutes you devote to being still in thought and movement. It is such a precious time for you, because you are allowing your mind to process thoughts and your body to calm its nervous system. You can embrace quiet time when you are winding down for bed at night, or if you're an early riser, first thing in the morning. And if that doesn't work, take a moment for yourself during the day whenever you can.

- Say an affirmation out loud or to yourself when you're in moments of distress, such as, *I am going to get through this hard time.*

- Say an affirmation out loud every morning, such as, *I will have a good day.*

- Grab a sticky notepad and write down the affirmations that you want to focus on. Place them in areas that you frequent around your home, such as a bathroom mirror. Constantly reading these affirmations in your home will encourage your mind to recognize these statements as true.

- If using sticky notes isn't ideal for you, set affirmations as calendar reminders in your phone so they pop up each day.

The affirmations you find in this journal can be said once or as many times as you need throughout the day.

How to Manifest Your Goals with Affirmations

Manifesting isn't about using magic to get what you want; it's about aligning yourself with the desires of your heart. While there are many key elements to manifesting your goals, affirmations are an essential part of that process. Remember, when manifesting, you must be intentional, ask your higher power directly for what you want, write down your goals, make moves toward those goals, be grateful, and release any limited thinking. Affirmations can help you do all that. Let's break it down:

1. First off, you must intentionally choose statements that speak directly to whatever you are trying to manifest—only you know what that is. Listen to your intuition, sis.

2. Next, ask your God or the universe for what you want to achieve. You can do this by saying it out loud, writing it down, or any other way you prefer.

3. Now, use that chosen affirmation to align your mind and heart with your future goal by repeating it to yourself until it sinks in and feels like the truth. While doing this, be sure to maintain an attitude of thankfulness for your present and future life: It will make a welcoming space for your desires to enter. You may not be where you want to be, but by using a positive statement to begin changing your mindset, you are shifting your spirit energetically toward that goal.

4. Use affirmations to overcome obstacles along the way. Affirmations promote shaking off any limited beliefs that could hinder you from achieving your goal, such as encouraging you to remain present while making steps toward your desired accomplishment.

Why Journaling Affirmations Is an Important Practice

Journaling affirmations creates space for you to process what you are trying to manifest in your life. Your thoughts impact your feelings and behaviors, so there is power in journaling. When you put your thoughts to paper, you will begin to see a change in yourself. In addition, journaling affirmations allows you to track your progress as you work toward your goals.

Most importantly, journaling is a great tool to help you manage your mental and emotional health. There is power in expressing what is going on in your mind on paper. When you're able to get all the thoughts and feelings that are going on in your head out into your journal, you can clearly evaluate what is truly going on with you. You'll be able to work through your emotional and mental well-being because journaling increases your ability to regulate your emotions by processing your thoughts and feelings so they don't manifest as detrimental habits. It's not good to keep all those feelings bottled up. Put them on paper so they can be set free and out of your mind, body, and soul.

The simple act of journaling about your affirmation will also help you figure out how the affirmation uniquely applies to you while also cementing its validity in your mind. Ask yourself these reflective questions: *Does this affirmation speak to a particular area of my life that I want to improve? Am I having a hard time believing this affirmation?* If you answer yes to both questions, then you've identified an affirmation that you can begin to use and explore in more depth in your journal. What area of your life does it speak to and why? If you answer no, you can use your journal to examine the ways you are currently living out that affirmation.

Take note of the wellness practices that are already helping you propel forward.

Additionally, this book is directed at Black women for a reason. Journaling provides you with a routine. Routines are powerful in helping you maintain your self-care practice. As a Black woman, actively choosing to elevate your wellness through self-care is a power move. Journaling affirmations gives you the space to figure out your unique identity, dreams, desires, and purpose. It allows you to channel your energy toward your goals so that your daily responsibilities and difficult situations don't cause you to lose sight of what you want to accomplish. So, for example, when you've had a long day or week of experiencing microaggressions, spending time with yourself journaling will help you stop the oppression you experience from eating you up inside and ruining your health. Therefore, *Affirmations for Black Women: A Journal* is essential to your radical self-care practice.

Affirmations

I am ready to connect to my higher self.

Your higher self is the wisest version of your inner being. When you are connected to your higher self, your intuition is strong and guides you to the things that are in alignment with your life's path. Preparing yourself for what you are trying to manifest is the first step. Use this affirmation to ready your mind, body, and soul with what you want to accomplish, sis. By telling yourself that you are ready to connect to your higher self, you are calling in energy that will help you propel forward and letting your God and/or the universe know that you are intentional about vibrating at new levels. Use the following space to explore attributes of your higher self.

I recognize rest as a form of self-love.

Taking time to rest is not only one of the best forms of self-love but also your greatest resistance in a society that has convinced Black women that we need to overwork ourselves to experience love. Rest up, sis. You cannot be the best version of yourself if you are *tiredt*. If you find it hard to prioritize rest, use the following space to explore why you think you don't deserve space to chill out. And if this isn't an issue for you, write about how rest has helped you.

....
....
....
....
....
....
....
....
....
....
....
....
....
....
....
....
....

I believe the life I want is within my reach.

Believe it and you will achieve it. Simple, right? The structure of the world tells you that what you want to do is not within your range. Because, as Black women, we often witness others have lived experiences that we can only imagine. Shake off this mindset. Repeat to yourself: *I believe the life I want is within my reach.* So, what do you want? Let it all out in the following space. There is power in writing it plain so you can see it and then believe it.

....

....

....

....

....

....

....

....

....

....

....

....

....

....

....

....

....

I already have all the qualities to be successful.

That's right: You already have all the qualities it takes to be successful. Now, the question is, do you believe this? Seriously. If you find yourself questioning your skills to accomplish great things, ask yourself where that thought is coming from and who told you that. Because, girl, you were born with the ability to smash all your goals. Tell impostor syndrome to *shhh*. Journal about your innate skills that will help you be a total success.

I attract people who will help me succeed.

As you work toward your goals, you will need people to help you on this journey. They might be acquaintances, friends, family, coworkers, mentors, etc. You may not know who your supporters will be, but what's important is that you open your energy to attract the right helpers. You don't have to do it all alone. Remove that strong, independent Black woman badge. Journal about the kind of people you would like to attract to assist with your achievements.

I don't have to be a strong Black woman.

It's time to put your cape down. Being a "strong Black woman" is played out. This trope is rooted in centuries of oppression. You are allowed to live a soft life (one with the least stress and resistance). In this lifestyle, you do things like no longer prioritizing everyone else's needs while ignoring your own. You're a boundary baddie—write about ways that you can release being a strong Black woman and embrace a life of ease.

I release feelings of guilt around my self-care.

Practicing self-care is essential to maintaining your well-being. But sometimes, you may harbor feelings of guilt around it. Many Black women are conditioned by our lived experiences to believe that we do not have the right to engage in self-love practices. So, when you do, you feel guilty and stop practicing self-care. Take time now to let go of your feelings of remorse. You are worthy of care. Explore the reasons behind your guilt in the following space.

I am responsible for my personal development.

The power is all yours when it comes to your own personal development. Oppressive societal systems will attempt to strip you of your autonomy when it pertains to your well-being. Take a stand and take your power back. Do not allow other people's actions or opinions to influence how you choose to improve yourself. Everybody will have something to say. Ignore the chatter and feel empowered to take ownership of your life's advancement. What are ways you can take responsibility for your personal growth? Journal about them in the following space.

I am secure in my current life decisions.

Society will try to tell you how to live your life as a Black woman. Do not listen. Your choices in life are unique to your liking. And because you are the one who must live with your life decisions, it's imperative that you trust your choice-making skills. This will open more doors for what you are manifesting and build up your self-confidence. Evaluate what's going on in your life. Are you secure in your current life decisions? If yes, write about it in the following space. If no, use this space to explore why.

....

....

....

....

....

....

....

....

....

....

....

....

....

....

....

....

....

I am committed to my emotional healing.

Emotional healing is very important for practicing radical self-care. However, it is not always a fun experience. As you heal emotionally, you will encounter painful emotions that you will not want to address. Resist the impulse to dismiss these feelings. Your healing matters. At your own pace, commit to your emotional healing. It will improve your mental health and better your mind for your manifestations. What are some things that you need to heal from emotionally? Write about them in the following space.

My worth isn't defined by my hair length.

No matter how long or short you decide to wear your hair, you are beautiful and deserving of love and admiration. Societal beauty standards feed you the message that having long hair makes you prettier and more feminine. If you have shorter hair, this can cause you to question your beauty. If you have longer hair, you may cling to it as a source of validation. And while your hair is a source of pain and pride, it doesn't define your worth as a person. Your hair, however you decide to style it, is magnificent because it's yours. Explore what your hair means to you in the following space.

....

....

....

....

....

....

....

....

....

....

....

....

....

....

....

....

I am careful with where I focus my energy.

Existing as a Black woman is exhausting. That's why it's important to be careful with where you focus your energy. Think of your energy as a budget. Spend too much time on things that are not aligned with your manifestations, and you will lose sight of your goals with zero energy to work toward them. Evaluate how you've been using your energy and brainstorm ways to manage it in the following space.

My value is not wrapped up in my job.

Society wants to make you believe that your worth is tied to your job. This is because the world places more value on the things you do as a Black woman than who you are as a person. If you find yourself beginning to believe that how you perform at your job is linked to your self-worth, then you need to use this affirmation. It's a great reminder that you are more than your occupation. Explore your thoughts on how much value you place on identity in relation to career, and examine if you have been linking your worth to your actions versus who you are in the following space.

....
....
....
....
....
....
....
....
....
....
....
....
....
....
....
....
....

I am allowed to experience joy in the middle of pain.

When you're going through a hard time, it can sometimes feel like a betrayal of your pain to experience joy. Take a deep breath, release it, and tell yourself that you deserve happiness in the middle of life's difficulties. Resist letting your stressors convince you that you must sit in misery. Take the time now to write about something that recently filled your spirit with joy.

I am not afraid to use my voice to speak my truth.

Speaking up for yourself can be frightening, but it's essential to your self-care. Society has worked hard to convince Black women that what we have to say doesn't matter. Or that our tone and intention in speech are wrong. Don't let that stop you. Using your voice to speak your truth in all situations will increase your peace and self-confidence. Think about something that you've been needing to get off your chest. Let it all out in the following space.

....
....
....
....
....
....
....
....
....
....
....
....
....
....
....
....
....
....
....

I am healing from past relationship traumas.

Building strong and healthy relationships includes healing from past traumatic experiences. It's important to make sure the dysfunctional dynamics of your previous relationships do not impact your current bonds. However, healing doesn't have a timeline. All that matters is that you are doing the work. Think of someone who has hurt you and how that connection negatively impacts your life. Then explore how you can heal from this.

I am working on expressing my emotions.

The world has made it very clear that it does not care about the emotional well-being of Black women. For many of us, ignoring our feelings and biting our tongues when it comes to expressing our emotions is second nature. This creates a disconnection with your inner self and causes you to be uncomfortable with sitting in or sharing your emotions. Use this affirmation as a declaration to give yourself space to say how you truly feel. Write about those feelings in the following space.

I consume foods that are kind to my body.

Self-care requires you to listen to your body. What you eat impacts your mind and body. And with preventable diseases being the leading cause of illnesses in Black women, there's no better time than the present to affirm practicing healthy eating habits to help you reach your wellness goals. Only you know what kinds of foods your body does or doesn't like. The more you eat foods that are kind to your body, the better you will feel. Pay attention and journal about how you can be more mindful about what you put into your body.

....
....
....
....
....
....
....
....
....
....
....
....
....
....
....
....
....

I can manage my time better to reach my goals.

Trying to manifest the life that you want will require you to buckle down and do some planning. This includes managing your time. As you assent to your goals, you will want to make sure that you are using your free time wisely. Now, this doesn't mean you should pack your calendar with things that are only related to what you want to achieve. It means respecting your time so that you are not overworked or stressed out about reaching your future accomplishments. Consider making space at the end of your day or cutting back on something, like watching too much TV. Think about how you can better manage your time. Plan in the following space.

I will not compare my body to others.

The world is cruel to Black women's bodies. From childhood, we are demon-ized, sexualized, and criticized. You then internalize the negative narratives about your body and are tempted to compare yours to other women— obsessing over how you could have a better shape. This is detrimental to your mental health. It lowers your self-esteem and morphs the reality of how you view yourself. It's time to learn to love the temple you are in. Explore the things you like about your body in the following space. And if you find this hard to do, explore why you feel the need to compare your body to others.

I am aligned with the desires of my heart.

When practicing radical self-care and manifestation, it's important to align yourself with the desires of the heart. Doing this allows the universe and/or your God to know that you are serious about what you want. Take the time now to jot down what you are wanting to manifest, and explore whether your thoughts and actions are aligned with what you want to achieve.

I release feelings of shame around my past.

Shame is one of the most damaging emotions to take hold in your body. It can paralyze you with fear of moving forward in life. The truth is this: We all have things we are ashamed about from our past. But whatever you did, girl, you did it out of survival and ignorance—you don't know what you don't know. Forgive your former self, and release those feelings of shame. Journal about any shameful memories that you are struggling to let go of.

....
....
....
....
....
....
....
....
....
....
....
....
....
....
....
....

I forgive those who have hurt me.

Unforgiveness is a heavy burden for your soul, sis. It's time to let go of your past hurt. For your mind's and soul's well-being, it's important to make an effort to forgive people. This doesn't excuse whatever pain or trauma they may have inflicted on you. Forgiveness is about not allowing the actions of others to create mental and emotional blocks in your life. Is there someone you need to work on forgiving? Write about it.

I embrace my happiness without suspicion.

You deserve to experience happiness. When you've been taught that pleasure only comes after pain, you find it hard to embrace joyful experiences. Being suspicious of your bliss questions the power of your ability to manifest and rejects the gift that whatever the higher entity you believe in has sent. This causes you to focus your energy on negativity instead of on what is bringing you cheer. Sis, embrace your happiness without suspicion. It will call more good things into your life. What is something that currently makes you happy? Write about it.

I am allowed to be my authentic self.

Give yourself permission to show up in the world as the most authentic version of yourself. From childhood to now, you have probably had many experiences that taught you to suppress your true feelings and thoughts. That's because the world rejects and demeans Black women for simply existing. So, it is self-care for you to be who you are and not who you think you should be. What are ways that you can practice showing up as your most authentic self? Explore this in the space that follows.

My work ethic is more than enough.

It's time to shatter the mindset of having to work twice as hard to get half as far. This sets you up to believe that you are not a hard worker. Whatever level of effort you put in is sufficient. You are dealing with a lot as a Black woman, such as constant pressure from the world and your peers to solve everybody's problems. Enough is enough. Decide to affirm that your work ethic is more than enough. Explore the relationship between your work ethic and the way you view yourself in the following space.

I give myself grace as I reach my goals.

Give yourself the same grace that you give others. You must be gentle with yourself as you accomplish great things. Those goals of yours require a lot of effort. When you give yourself grace, you learn the power of being kind to yourself. Give yourself permission to have many chances at achieving greatness. You deserve it. What are some ways that you can practice showing grace to yourself? Brainstorm in the following space.

How others perceive me doesn't define me.

Being a Black woman means hypervisibility is expected. People are always looking at you because you are often one of the few Black women in the room. And sometimes, this can impact the way you think about yourself. Recognize that how others perceive you does not define who you are as a person. What others think about you is not your responsibility. What you believe about yourself is all that matters. Express your thoughts about your unique self in the following space.

I am open to all paths that lead me to my goals.

There are endless possibilities of how you can see your desires come to fruition. To manifest your dreams, you must be willing to reach your achievements through different avenues. This decreases limited thinking and creates space for abundance in your life. Grant yourself permission to be open to all paths that lead to your goals. You won't regret it. Do you struggle with keeping an open mind regarding your goals? Explore this in the following space.

I let people be themselves.

The secret to creating long-lasting connections is to let others be themselves, believe what you see, and decide if you want to engage. This helps you align with those who are meant to be in your life. Sis, you gotta remember: The right relationships propel you toward your goals. Use this affirmation to help you radically accept that you can't control other people. You can only control your level of engagement with them. Write about ways you can practice this.

I let go of impostor syndrome.

Impostor syndrome is when you believe your successes are not deserved. The root of impostor syndrome is feeling anxious and insecure. It is a very common feeling for Black women as a lot of the rooms we enter don't necessarily want us to be there. But it's time for you to let that go. Everything that you accomplished, *you did that*, and you deserve to be praised for it. When's the last time impostor syndrome crept up on you? How did you handle it? What are ways that you can deal with impostor syndrome in the future? Journal about your experiences.

I can say no.

That's right. You have the right to say no without an explanation. When you say yes or maybe but really mean no, you are ignoring your own needs and boundaries. Sometimes, we fear saying no because we don't want to disappoint others. Honor yourself by affirming you will be honest with yourself and others when you want to say no to something. Do you have a hard time telling others no because of guilt? Dig deep into this in the following space by examining your feelings around saying no.

I take time to explore my purpose.

It is important that you take your time with exploring your purpose in life. The world will try to rush you in a direction, but resist it. Tap in to your intuition. You want to follow the path that the higher entity you believe in is calling you to. If you're struggling with figuring out your purpose, ask yourself these questions: *What makes me happy? What do I like? Why do I like it? What are my core values? Does what I want to do align with those core values?* Write your answers in the following space, and come back to these questions as frequently as you need.

My identity is not found in my trauma and pain.

The world loves to define Black women by our pain. It is as if your hardships are part of your identity. But this is not true. You are more than that. If you've had traumatic experiences, know that you did not deserve to go through that hurt. What happened to you does not define you. Choose to let it go. Set yourself free from the burden of your pain by writing about it.

I love who I am becoming.

You are a work in progress, and as you get closer to your goals, it's important to acknowledge the person you are becoming. You may not be where you want to be, but you're not where you used to be either, sis. That's an accomplishment that deserves recognition. Take the time now to explore who you are becoming and write a letter to her praising her for all her personal growth.

I am patient with myself.

It's important for you to be patient with yourself as you work toward your goals. Manifesting things takes time. To be patient is to be compassionate, and you deserve to experience self-compassion. You live in a world that doesn't believe in giving women who look like you more than one chance. Don't adopt this belief. There isn't a set pace for the progress of your accomplishments. What are ways that you can practice being more patient with yourself? Write about them.

I am allowed to start over.

Give yourself permission to hit the reset button on life whenever you need it. Listen, you might have been encouraged to stick to the first path you chose in different areas of your life. This is because you were made to believe that you do not have access to an infinite number of opportunities. But the truth is, Black women are the archetype of starting over. It's ancestral. What is something in your life that needs a do-over? Write about it.

My hair is beautiful and unique.

The way you choose to wear your hair (natural, locked, protected, relaxed, etc.) is beautiful because it is uniquely yours. The world will always attempt to make you think negatively about your hair texture. Drown 'em out. Proudly embrace a part of you that is exclusive to you as a Black woman. Only queens can rock that crown of yours. What do you love about your hair? List them out. It's important for your well-being to show appreciation for your hair.

....
....
....
....
....
....
....
....
....
....
....
....
....
....
....
....
....
....

I will no longer overextend myself.

In life, Black women are expected to have the capacity to do everything. You may feel pressured to take on more than you should to protect the perception of your identity. Stop that. It is exhausting to your mind, body, and soul. Girl, put your needs first and only commit to what you want. Explore the ways you have overextended yourself in the past, and brainstorm how you can change this behavior in the future.

I embrace movement as a form of healing.

Prioritize your wellness by reframing exercise as essential movement for your body. Moving your body at least once a day for an extended period is healing. It allows you to release any stored-up emotions living in your body (like annoyance from a microaggression). You need this. Take the time to think about how you can include movement into your daily life, and write your ideas in the following space.

....

....

....

....

....

....

....

....

....

....

....

....

....

....

....

....

....

....

I release my desire to be perfect.

As a Black woman, you feel the pressure to be perfect so you can gain respect or accomplish anything. Sis, perfectionism is just anxiety in action. You are trying to control the outcome of a situation by attempting to do everything flawlessly. Let it go. It's causing distress. Explore in the following space what being perceived as perfect means to you and how you can practice releasing this desire.

I treat my body with kindness.

Just living can be hard on your body—especially as a Black woman. The world is tough on you, so treat yourself with some compassion. Being kind to your body means not shaming or criticizing it for not meeting unrealistic Eurocentric beauty standards. Your body is yours and it's helping you live wonderfully. Write down some things you love about your body.

I am not afraid of the next level.

As you continue to use affirmations, your life will change. You will elevate to higher levels—internally and externally. When your life is marked by the experience of oppression, limited beliefs can take root in the mind. You become comfortable with the present and fear the future. Let it go and trust your ability to adjust to the life you're creating. Write down what you're afraid of and speak courage over it.

....

....

....

....

....

....

....

....

....

....

....

....

....

....

....

....

....

....

I attract healthy friendships with Black women.

Having healthy relationships with other Black women is essential to your living experience. These close bonds help encourage and maintain your higher vibrational level of self. But sometimes, it can be hard to find these long-lasting and emotionally safe friendships. Shift your thinking by using this affirmation so that you can attract the right sistahs into your life. What do you want your friendships to look like? Explore this in the following space.

My inner child deserves to be loved.

Your inner child needs care. She was stripped of her innocence because society sees little Black girls as adults. Thus, you may have developed the belief that you don't deserve tender loving care. Tap back in to the pureness of being a child and love on her. This will help you heal as you ascend to the next level of self. Write a love letter to your inner child. She needs to read it.

I give myself grace and space to heal.

Sometimes, we want to rush our healing. But the fact is, you need time. It can take years to shed the effects of previous traumas, such as the negative thoughts you've adopted about yourself because of misogynoir. You need to be gentle with yourself. There is no specific timeline to address your inner healing. Make time now to journal about the things you need to heal from.

I release all forms of self-criticism.

Criticism feels comfortable when you're used to your existence being nit-picked by the world. You're taught that things like your hair, body, and voice need to be altered for you to be accepted. However, judging every aspect of yourself doesn't fix anything. It only decreases your self-esteem. Let's get real: There is nothing wrong with you. Everything about you is beautiful. Boost your self-worth by writing down everything about you that you love. Release your need to self-criticize.

I make space to be vulnerable with myself and others.

Vulnerability is the key to building stronger relationships. Being vulnerable means that you are open and honest about your emotions with yourself and others. Unfortunately, you live in a world where Black women are not allowed to display softer emotions without being criticized. You're encouraged to maintain a strong persona by neglecting your feelings. But the gag is, vulnerability is a strength. What are some ways that you can be more open with yourself and others? Write them out.

I don't need to experience trauma to recognize my strength.

What doesn't kill you doesn't make you stronger: It traumatizes you. And as a result, you create beliefs and behaviors that do you more harm than good. You've been taught that the only way you can recognize your strength is to experience hardships. And while tough times help you realize your resiliency, it's not necessary to access your inner baddie. Your power already exists within you. Use this affirmation to declare that you will not dismiss your pain for the sake of becoming a stronger person. In this space, address any pain you are carrying, giving it the acknowledgment it deserves.

I am allowed to be angry.

Think about the last time something made you angry. Did you allow yourself to feel this emotion? If you answered no, then listen up. Too often, we are worried about being perceived as the "Angry Black Woman," even when our rage is a justifiable response to mistreatment. And let's be real: There's *a lot* to be mad about in this world. It is okay to experience and express your aggravation. Free yourself from the fear of the negative connotation of being angry as a Black woman. Use the following space to explore your thoughts and feelings about something that made you angry.

I de-center my life around romantic relationships.

Society works overtime to convince you that your purpose is to get married and have children. This can cause you to become obsessed with finding a life partner. However, locating said lover is not easy for Black women. So, you remain single and searching. You are not a failure because you haven't found your forever boo. There is freedom in de-centering your life around dating. When you are too focused on finding love instead of loving yourself and fostering the other relationships in your life, you lose sight of the things you value. How can you work on removing romantic relationships from the center of your life? Explore this in the following space.

I love the color of my skin.

Sis, your skin is beautiful. Don't let anybody tell you otherwise. I know that sometimes there is a burden that comes with living in your skin. People treat you differently. They try to make you think your worth is of lesser value because you walk around in melanated skin. They make assumptions and attempt to ruin your day with microaggressions because of your skin color. And if you have internalized these negative messages, you can begin to hate the skin that you're in. Let's put a stop to that. Whether you're a light-skinned, brown-skinned, or dark-skinned Black woman, be proud of the color of your skin. It's beautiful. Use the following space to reflect on the reasons you love being a *Brown-Skinned Girl*.

I am breaking generational curses by healing myself.

It's not easy doing the work of healing yourself to break the patterns of inter-generational trauma (a.k.a. generational curses). However, it is very neces-sary. Intergenerational trauma (example: emotional neglect) is trauma that is passed down to you from those who came before you, such as parents, grandparents, and even the collective Black community. The previous expe-riences of others aren't yours to own. However, the way you were socialized in the world is directly impacted by the preceding generations. And if the effects of intergenerational trauma go unchecked, they can hold you back in every area of your life. Take a moment right now to write out the unhealthy generational patterns in your family (examples: communication or parenting styles) and how you plan to break them.

....

....

....

....

....

....

....

....

....

....

....

....

I let go of my desire for struggle love.

"Struggle love" is the belief that for a couple to become stronger in their relationship, one or both must cause mental, physical, and/or emotional harm to the other. For a lot of Black women, "struggle love" is synonymous with romance. We are expected to endure disrespect from partners to prove that we are worthy of being loved. Do not allow the way the world views Black women and our dating lives to dictate the kind of love you deserve. Embrace experiencing romance that is filled with respect. Use the following space to explore what experiencing love that isn't "struggle love" would look like for you.

....
....
....
....
....
....
....
....
....
....
....
....
....
....

I deserve a doctor who listens to me.

The quality of medical care that Black women receive is tainted by misogynoir. Often, we are misdiagnosed, with our health concerns ignored. And when your wellness needs are unmet, you may become discouraged from taking care of yourself. Take your power back. You deserve a medical provider who listens to and collaborates with you. Write about how you felt during your last negative interaction with a doctor. Explore how you'll advocate for your health at your next appointment.

....

....

....

....

....

....

....

....

....

....

....

....

....

....

....

....

....

My body is a safe space.

The world will villainize your Blackness and try to make you believe your existence is a problem. It is not. Fight back against this false belief created from society's projection by making your inner being a safe environment for your mental and emotional needs. Use the following space to release any anxious or intrusive thoughts about yourself.

I am open to all streams of income.

The truth is there is a wage gap for Black women. But don't let this discourage you from calling in an abundant bank account. Believe that you can have access to multiple streams of income. By using this affirmation, you are releasing any limiting beliefs you have about money. You will shift the way you view your finances—seeing it as a helpful tool instead of a burden. Explore your feelings about money in the following space.

I deserve to experience Black girl joy.

There's regular joy, and then there's Black girl joy. Black girl joy is rooted in you unapologetically living in your full Black womanhood and not allowing the experiences of oppression to impact your inner glow. You deserve to experience joy as often as you can. Life does not always need to be marked by trauma. Use this affirmation to ignite the joy that lives within. What's something that brings you joy? Write about it.

I will not lower my standards to experience romance.

Dating as a Black woman is hard. Colorism, racism, and fetishism can sometimes be big obstacles to experiencing partnership. And so, you may be tempted to give the first person a chance who seems decent but doesn't meet all your non-negotiables. Don't do it, sis. Lowering your romantic standards also means settling for lower vibrational experiences. You deserve the best. Explore the traits you want in an ideal partner in the following space.

I no longer compare my life to others.

In the age of social media, it can be tempting to tap in to what others are doing with their lives and compare it to yours. Doing this will rob you of your Black girl joy, lowering your feelings of self-worth. You are more than what you haven't yet accomplished. Your life is on its own timeline designed by a universal force. Take the time to examine whose timeline you are on: yours or your higher power's.

I prioritize making time for my self-care.

Putting yourself first is the key to maintaining your well-being. It can sometimes feel like making space for you to practice self-care is impossible. However, if you *choose* to prioritize it, you can make it happen. And as a Black woman, you can't afford to not create time for your needs. You live in a world that expects you to do the exact opposite. Use this affirmation to begin brainstorming how you can move your self-care to the top of your to-do list.

I can detach from unhealthy relationships.

Whether it's a family member, romantic partner, friend, or coworker, you have the capacity to detach from relationships that are unhealthy. Breaking bonds that are not good for us can be hard. You may fear hurting the other person's feelings or dealing with the loss of that relationship. Sis, you carry a lot on your shoulders on the daily. And to get to the next level of your life, you need to set yourself free from people who are bringing you down. Take time now to write about any relationships that are causing you distress.

I choose to unlearn negative self-talk.

Your self-talk shapes the way you see yourself. And if you've internalized the negative things society says about Black women, you probably catch yourself engaging in negative self-talk several times a week or more. Stop being your worst critic. You are doing better than you think. Choose to change your inner self-dialogue to be more positive. Explore the frequent negative thoughts you have about yourself and challenge the validity of them in the following space.

My relationship status does not dictate my worth.

We live in a world that likes to measure a woman's worth by her marital status with marriage holding high social currency. Recent statistics say that more Black women are single than any other race. This is often used to validate the belief that as a Black woman you are less desirable. *False.* Whether you're single or have a partner, your relationship status does not dictate your worth. Learn to find value in who you are outside of a partnership. Explore your feelings on this in the following space.

I allow myself to feel and release my sadness.

If something has got you down lately, sis, allow yourself to feel it and then release it. There is power in allowing your sadness to say hello and good-bye. As a Black woman, you probably have stored-up emotions with sadness being one of the strongest ones. Letting this emotion go will decrease the likelihood of it manifesting in your body as trauma. Use the following space to pour your heart out about something that hurt you. Let it go.

I have the power to validate myself.

The world will do its best to invalidate your experiences as a Black woman, making you think the things you live through (like microaggressions) are not real. This is an attempt to strip you of the power of your existence. So, you must be able to validate yourself. It's essential to your personal growth to feel seen and understood by the most important person in your life: *you*. Use this affirmation to help regulate your emotions and increase your self-confidence so you remain focused on your well-being and manifestations. Journal about a time someone shut you down about something you experienced.

I will not allow society to dictate my actions.

At some point in your life, you've probably thought, *If I change this about myself, I will receive better treatment from others.* The truth is, you can't allow society's standards to influence the way you move through life. Things are always changing, and it is exhausting to keep up with these changes—especially in a world that is designed to oppress women who look like you. So, girl, focus on yourself and resist conforming to society's unrealistic expectations of living. Form your own unique identity. Muse about who that girl is in the following space.

....

....

....

....

....

....

....

....

....

....

....

....

....

....

....

I will get through this hard time.

Use this affirmation to motivate you as you experience any present hardships. When you're going through it, sometimes you don't believe that life will get better. That's your mind trying to convince you that your life is sedentary. That's not true. Know that life is constantly moving, and while what you're currently experiencing may be wreaking havoc on your well-being, it will eventually pass. Take the time now to journal about the things that are causing you distress. Use this affirmation and space to process your emotions and thoughts.

My fears do not control me.

Fear can paralyze the mind, body, and soul. It holds you back from pursuing your dreams. While some fears are reality-based, most fears are created by the mind. When you're crippled with fear, you lack trust in self. Trust that you will be able to emotionally and physically withstand any obstacle that gets thrown in your way. Girl, you're resilient. Tell yourself: *I can do anything I put my mind to. My fears do not control me.* What is something that you're afraid of that you need to work on letting go? Write about it.

I can ask others for help.

You don't have to go through life alone. You are allowed to ask others for help. Seeking assistance for your needs makes you a brilliant person because you recognize that it requires inner strength to accept support. The world wants to convince you that you don't deserve care and that only depending on yourself will get you further. This is false. It'll only lead to an unfulfilling and lonely life. Do you have a hard time asking for help? Explore this in the following space.

I choose to not believe the lies of discrimination.

Experiencing discrimination is traumatizing and exhausting. It requires a lot of energy to recover from it. And whether it's overt or covert misogynoir, it still hurts. It is meant to make you feel less than. And if you're not careful, you will take in these painful experiences and believe that your existence does not matter. Choose to not believe the lies of discrimination. You are more than enough. Your life is of great value. What are some self-beliefs that you need to unlearn as a result of being on the receiving end of racism and sexism? Journal about them.

I am worthy of the life I want.

Part of manifesting your desires to fruition is believing that you are worthy of experiencing them. Do you believe you are worthy of the life that you want? You might not feel like you are because of how the world treats you, but you most definitely deserve the life of your dreams. If you struggle with self-worth, explore why you think you don't deserve the things you desire, and what makes you uniquely worthy of these desires.

I forgive myself for my past mistakes.

Forgiving others is optional, but forgiving yourself is mandatory. It can be hard to move forward in life if you are holding on to your past mistakes. What purpose does it serve you to do that? None. It lives as an excuse to not try to work toward your goals. Set your soul free by learning to forgive your past mistakes. What from your past are you refusing to forgive yourself for? Explore this in the following space.

I practice being present in my relationships.

To foster strong relationships, you must practice being present. Being mindful of how you show up in your relationships means being able to hold space for those you are connected to. It also means allowing yourself to see the person for who they are and engage accordingly. This type of practice is important because it helps you place people in your life where they belong. You'll know who is an acquaintance and who is a good friend. Take stock of your current relationships in the following space. Think about ways that you can either begin to be, or maintain being, present in each one.

I celebrate all my wins.

Even if you've got nobody else to celebrate your wins with, celebrate them with yourself. Be proud of what you've done—no matter how small the accomplishment. You are a Black woman living in a society that has one goal: oppress you to oblivion. But you know what? *Still, you rise.* Take the time now to write about some of your recent wins. Go off!

I set my own beauty standard.

You have the power to set your own beauty standard. In a world where white European features are idolized, you must reject the messaging that your skin, hair, face, and body are not beautiful. You are a gorgeous individual, simply because the way you were made is unique to you. Resist the need to fit into whatever beauty ideals society praises. Explore what you find beautiful about yourself in the following space.

I trust everything will work out in my favor.

Creating your dream life requires trusting yourself and your higher power. Your life experiences will try to convince you that you are not worthy of good things. You may even question your own capabilities in reaching your goals. Stop that, sis. Use this affirmation to begin believing your current circumstances do not dictate your future. What's to come will be for your benefit. Explore the hopes you have for the future in the following space.

I will no longer betray my intuition.

Your intuition is your guiding light in this life. Ignoring it means betraying yourself. And betraying yourself means delaying your manifestations. As a Black woman, you have a strong intuition and have experienced many situations where you had to muffle its voice. Forgive yourself and move forward, declaring that you will be loyal to your instinct and no longer ignore any directives from your inner being. Take time now to journal about ways you can honor your intuition every day.

I give myself permission to grieve broken friendships.

The end of a friendship hits different than a breakup with a romantic partner. Whether it's a person or a group of people, this was a bond that you envisioned having in your life for a long time. It's imperative that you grieve this kind of deep loss. Mourning former friendships helps you move forward and create other meaningful connections that elevate your life so you don't fall into the trap of being a hyper-independent Black woman. Give yourself permission to heal from these broken bonds. Explore your feelings about your most recent friendship that ended.

The more I heal, the better I feel.

Healing your inner self is not easy, but it is necessary. It's what will help you clear your mind and manifest your dreams. Healing lets the universe and any higher power you believe in know that you are making room for what's to come. And while healing from past traumas and hurts can really sting, the more you work through these things, the better you will eventually feel. What are some things you need to heal from that might be holding you back? What would it be like to no longer carry these wounds? Write about this.

My failures are not a reflection of my worth.

Learning to deal with failures and not internalize them is part of your self-care journey. Your failures are not a reflection of your worth. You are Black excellence simply because you exist. Do not allow your external experience to convince you otherwise. Your value is not measured by your successes. Choose to see your letdowns as lessons and insight into how you can move closer to your goals. How do you feel when you flop at something? Journal about the false beliefs about self that are created by the times you've failed.

My weight does not define me.

Society puts pressure on you to look a certain way, especially regarding your weight. If you let it, that number on the scale can send you into a shame-filled spiral. This can cause you to have low self-esteem and distract you from your future. Resist unrealistic body standards by fighting a fixation on weight. Your worth is not defined by how much you weigh. It's defined by how much you love yourself. What does your relationship with your weight look like? How has this impacted your life? Explore this relationship and its effects in the following space.

My energy is magnetic, and I attract good things.

Having good energy will attract good things to your life. Use this affirmation to help call in all that you are hoping to achieve. Your energy plays a part in helping you manifest your dreams. While it's important to have magnetic energy, it's also important to make sure that you are only trying to attract positive things. What kinds of things do you wish to attract into your life? Journal about them.

I trust that I am on the right path.

It's time to trust that your life is headed in the right direction. You're probably thinking, *But how do I know for sure?* You don't, but that's the beauty of actively practicing radical self-care. The more you do it, the more you become self-confident and embrace your ability to let go and let your higher power do what it do. Trusting that you are on the right path means believing that you have the tools to face whatever life throws at you. Do you feel good about where your life is going? If yes, write about this. If not, brainstorm ways you can get your life on the preferred track.

I am grateful for past and future successes.

Be grateful for your past and future successes, as this energy creates space for you to experience abundance. You've been told that you must work twice as hard to get half as far. Thus, you become a high achiever, which causes you to be laser-focused on your future goals and ignore (much less enjoy) your current or past accomplishments. Girl, this cycle is exhausting. Find solace in gratitude. Take the time now to celebrate all that you have achieved and will achieve. Write about your accomplishments here.

I don't wait for opportunities; I create them.

Black women are not given the same chances as non-Black women to build a thriving life and career. Don't worry: You have the power to create your own success story. Actively creating opportunities for yourself to reach your goals will shift your mindset. You will see your obstacles as a redirection and not a limitation. Now, list out your goals and explore what you have access to right now to help you achieve them.

....

....

....

....

....

....

....

....

....

....

....

....

....

....

....

....

....

I let go of survival mode.

Many Black women are living in survival mode. Every day, you are burdened with the responsibility of protecting your psyche from the pain of misogynoir. While helpful, this state of mind can also be harmful to your mental and emotional health as well as relationships. When you constantly move through life on the defensive, you neglect being present, suppress your needs, and live with limitations. Use the following space to explore ways you can operate outside of survival mode.

I am responsible for my own emotions.

The world tries to convince Black women to carry the weight of the world's problems on our shoulders. And because of this, you may think you are responsible for other people's emotional well-being, such as your family, friends, and coworkers. Doing this too often can result in emotional distress. Stop holding space for others before holding it for yourself. Think about whose emotions are burdening you and explore why you are putting others' needs before your own.

I have compassion for the old me.

If you look back at previous versions of yourself and think, *yikes*, this means you're growing and moving forward in life. To manifest the life that you want, you will have to continuously shed the old you. However, be sure to show your previous self some compassion. She may have been dealing with a lot—like grappling with internalized racism. Take time now to write kind words to her.

My version of Blackness is valid.

Whichever way you choose to present in this world as a Black woman is valid. Others' preconceived ideas about you as a person with melanin are none of your business. You are allowed to exist as an individual and not a representative of the collective. It's imperative that you show up however *you* want because this will help you build a stronger bond with your intuition—it guides you on your manifestation journey. What do you love about your version of Blackness? Write about it.

AFFIRMATION

I am gentle with myself through life's transitions.

It can be difficult to adjust to new transitions in life, so you must be gentle with yourself. You can't predict what kind of changes life will throw at you, but you can be certain that your resiliency will kick in and you'll be all right. Still, be gentle with yourself. Are there any current big or small life adjustments that you need to get used to? Examine your feelings about this.

....

....

....

....

....

....

....

....

....

....

....

....

....

....

....

....

....

....

....

I can learn the boundaries of my body.

Knowing the boundaries of your body means getting an understanding of what kind of touch you do and don't like. Personal growth requires that you be self-aware, and it includes figuring out your physical boundaries—from your head to your toes. For example, knowing what turns you on sexually or what triggers a negative emotional reaction. Do you know the boundaries of your body? If so, what are they? If not, explore what they may be.

I can create a new reality with my mind.

Believing that you can create a new reality with your mind is one of your first steps in manifesting your life goals. Your thoughts and feelings can turn into behaviors that either push you forward or hold you back in life. It's up to you to decide which direction you want to go in. Ask yourself: *What thoughts about myself and my current reality are preventing me from pursuing my purpose?* Use this journal prompt to help you begin shifting your mindset.

I am not afraid of being alone.

Never fear being alone because there's nothing more comforting than your own peace. When you are afraid of being alone, you are fearful of being abandoned by others, so you abandon yourself. You neglect your needs and betray your desires. This does not honor your true self and can throw you off track with your manifestations. So, get comfortable with your own solitude. Stop seeking unsatisfying relationships to fill a void because you are afraid of being alone. Does this hit home? Explore your feelings about loneliness and being alone in the following space.

....
....
....
....
....
....
....
....
....
....
....
....
....
....
....

I will not minimize my presence.

Your lived experiences have taught you that to protect your peace, you must shrink your existence. Uh, no. You do not have to do this anymore. Take up space, sis. You deserve to be seen and heard. How others react to you using your voice is none of your business. It's not your fault if others are intimidated by your effervescence. That's on them. You continue to do you. Journal about practical ways in which you can stop minimizing your presence in your everyday life.

I listen to what my body is telling me.

To elevate your wellness, it is important to stop ignoring your needs and listen to what your body is telling you. Breaking this habit will improve the relationship you have with yourself. Becoming self-aware increases your alignment with your manifestations. Your body sends you messages when it needs nourishment and restoration. What is your body currently telling you? Write about what it is saying.

I am allowed to be quiet.

Many Black women are expected to fit the loud and sassy friend stereotype. So, when you are quiet, others perceive you to be mean or rude. Do not allow others' projections to ruin your peace. You are allowed to be a quiet person. You do not have to uphold any characteristic stereotypes. The way others view your silence is their problem. Do you feel like you are allowed to be quiet? Or do you feel you must always speak up? Explore your feelings around this.

I am worthy of being loved.

Part of receiving love is believing that you deserve it. Living in an oppressive society will make you think you do not require love, so you reject the idea that you are even worthy of it. Cut it out, sis. Let people love on you. Do you struggle with feeling like you deserve to be loved? Think about where, when, and how you learned this. Who taught you that you don't deserve love? Write it out and get to the root so you can begin to accept the love you need.

I am engaged in reciprocal relationships.

Being in a relationship with someone (friend, family, coworker, partner, etc.) where you are the one who gives more energy than you receive is draining. You already face a world that is tough on you every day. You don't have time for connections where the other seemingly doesn't equally care about you. These kinds of bonds can also distract you from your goals and purpose. Let them go. Take the time in the following space to evaluate any relationships in your life where the energy exchange is not balanced.

I appreciate the things my body can do.

Your body can do amazing things, such as create life and keep you healthy. Learning to love the temple you're in isn't only about loving what's on the outside; it's also about appreciating what's on the inside. Take time to appreciate the times your body helped you beat an illness or signaled to you that it was time to rest. Think about all the magnificent things your body has done for you. Write about them and give thanks to that temple of yours.

I am not afraid of the real me.

The road to self-discovery is scary but enlightening. You get to meet the real you—the good, bad, and in-between. For so long, you've had to listen to the world tell you how to move through life as a Black woman. Now, it's time to listen to yourself. The more you practice self-care and journey through your manifestations, the better understanding you gain of yourself. You'll learn to accept the dynamic person that you are and not be afraid of the real you. Journal about the parts of you that you're afraid of but are ready to meet.

I am committed to positive thinking.

Committing to positive thinking means trying to focus on the good in any situation. This can be hard when your mind is hardwired to seek out negativity. But, listen up: You are entering a new era of your life. A space filled with intention. To see the powerful results of using affirmations, you are going to need to be intentional with your thinking. No matter what you're going through, honor the reality of the circumstance and embrace thinking positively when the time is right. Explore your thoughts on this practice and how it applies to your life.

I am devoted to my wellness.

Being devoted to your wellness is an act of resistance against an oppressive society, sis. You need to do this. By affirming that you will be dedicated to bettering your well-being, you are giving yourself permission to live a life of ease that is not centered around suffering. Your self-care habits will improve, and whatever you are manifesting will feel welcomed in your life. *Go you!* Explore ways that you can stay devoted to your wellness.

About the Author

OLUDARA ADEEYO is a psychotherapist and the author of *Self-Care for Black Women*. She is passionate about helping people, especially Black women, improve their overall wellness. Before becoming a clinical social worker, Oludara worked as a writer and editor. She has been an associate web editor at *Cosmopolitan* and the managing editor at *XXL*. Oludara lives in Los Angeles. *Affirmations for Black Women: A Journal* is her second book.